THE
POST- TRIBULATION
RAPTURE
OF THE
CHURCH

Also by Bob Mitchell

Rome, Babylon the Great and Europe

The Messiah Code

Antichrist, the Vatican and the Great Deception

Visit
Bob Mitchell's Blog at:
http://www. shofar-ministries.blogspot.co.uk/

Bob Mitchell DVDs at:
http://bibleprophecy-dvd-store.blogspot.co.uk/

(Shofar Ministries) YouTube channel at:
http://www.youtube.com/channel/UCjkZx8ouJVtxuIEFSbItFHA?

THE
POST-TRIBULATION
RAPTURE
OF THE
CHURCH

Bob Mitchell

THE POST-TRIBULATION RAPTURE OF THE CHURCH

Why I believe in the post-tribulation rapture.

I was a firm believer in a pre-trib rapture for several decades. I preached it as well as believed it. So why did I change my view?

What changed me was the sudden realisation that not only was I blindly accepting what I was being told the scriptures said regarding the rapture. But also, I became more aware that each of us are called to be Bereans to search the scriptures daily to see whether these things be so. We are also called to work out our salvation with fear and trembling.

I was doing neither of these things that are essential for our spiritual well-being.

What came as a real shock to me was there is no scripture from Genesis to Revelation that says Jesus will come secretly and remove the church before the final 7 years.

As a result of this and deeper study, I emerged a convinced believer in a post- tribulation rapture.

Arguments I put up against what I was finding fell apart. Arguments such as 1 Thess 5:9 "for God hath not appointed us to wrath, but to obtain salvation by our Lord Jesus Christ." Titus 2:13 "looking for that blessed hope, and the glorious appearing of the great God and our Saviour Jesus Christ;"
1 Thess 4:16-18 16 "for the Lord himself shall descend from heaven with a shout, with the voice of the archangel, and

with the trump of God: and the dead in Christ shall rise first then we which are alive and remain shall be caught up together with them in the clouds, to meet the Lord in the air: and so shall we ever be with the lord wherefore comfort one another with these words."

Rev 3:10 "because thou hast kept the word of my patience, I also will keep thee from the hour of temptation, which shall come upon all the world, to try them that dwell upon the earth."

As I studied these verses and others I was amazed to find these verses did not support a pre-tribulation rapture at all but when placed in context and looking at the Greek, which anyone can do today, they, more and more, took on a post-tribulation scenario rather than a pre-tribulation one.

Since that time I have become so convinced that the pre and mid-trib rapture theories are in error.

Also, many told me the post-trib position was a new teaching and that the church had always believed the rapture would take place at any moment and before the appearance of the Antichrist.

So I did some research for myself to see just how true these statements were. To my astonishment, I discovered a whole list of people who believed the Antichrist would come before the Lord Jesus returned for the church. A fact completely opposite to that which I had been told. Had these believers lied to me? No, I don't believe so. I believe they were sincere in what they said, but like me they had never checked to see if what they had been told was actually in the Bible.

Below is a list of teachers past and present who believed the church would see the Antichrist.

- John Calvin, Martin Luther, John Knox, John Bunyan, Isaac Newton, George Whitefield, Charles Hodge, Henry Alford, J.Sidlow Baxter,

- F.F. Bruce, Thomas Chalmers, Adam Clarke, Jonathan Edwards, Jim Elliott, W.J. Erdman, Robert Gundry, Matthew Henry, John Huss, Peter Marshall, Walter Martin,

- G.Campbell Morgan, George Mueller, Ian Murray, John Newton, H.J. Ockenga, Bernard Ramm, Demos Shakarian, A.B. Simpson,

- Oswald J. Smith, R.C.Sproul, Charles Spurgeon, Corrie Tenboom,

- S.P. Tragelles, William Tyndale, B.B. Warfield, Charles Wesley.

This doesn't mean post-trib is correct, but it does show it is not a new teaching in the church. It simply was never called post-trib because for them there was never a pre-trib.

So which rapture is scriptural? I want to use simple logic alongside scripture as we explore this subject without inserting anything that could be colouring my belief.

I was taught the church has expected the any moment imminent return of the Lord Jesus from the moment he ascended. Well has it?

IMMINENCE

Pre-trib teaches Christ could come at any moment. Nothing is needed to be fulfilled before Jesus raptures the church. Therefore, he could come at any moment. We are told the church has always believed in the imminent rapture of believers before the appearance of the Antichrist and the onset of the final 7 years or tribulation period.

Let us test this teaching...

Dr. Renald Showers, who is a believer in a pre-tribulation rapture, describes imminence as follows:

"An imminent event is one which is always 'hanging overhead, is constantly ready to befall or overtake one; close at hand in its incidence.' ('imminent,' The Oxford English Dictionary, 1901, V, 66.)

Thus, imminence carries the sense that it could happen at any moment. Other things may happen before the imminent event, but nothing else <u>must</u> take place before it happens."

If something else must take place before an event can happen, then that event is not imminent. In other words, the necessity of something else taking place first destroys the concept of imminency.

So if we discover Jesus had made predictions to individual believers or the church that had to happen after Christ's resurrection and ascension and before His return for the church the very discovery of such prophecies would make it obvious that the rapture was not imminent.

Why?

Because according to the above statement that would "destroy the concept of imminency."

Let's read Dr. Showers' statement again:

"If something else must take place before an event can happen, then that event is not imminent. In other words, the necessity of something else taking place first destroys the concept of imminency."

Over you see a timeline from 30 AD when the Lord Jesus died, was buried, rose again and ascended to heaven up to 96 AD when we believe John wrote the book of Revelation.

How could the early church have expected an any moment rapture when Jesus himself predicted.......

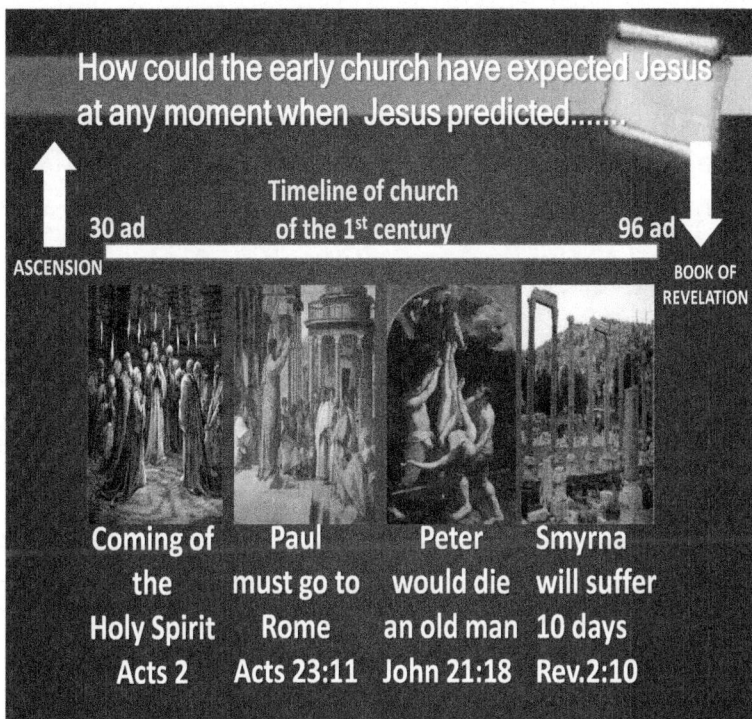

How could the early church have expected Jesus at any moment when Jesus predicted......

Timeline of church of the 1st century

30 ad — ASCENSION
96 ad — BOOK OF REVELATION

| Coming of the Holy Spirit | Paul must go to Rome | Peter would die an old man | Smyrna will suffer 10 days |
| Acts 2 | Acts 23:11 | John 21:18 | Rev.2:10 |

1. Before the Lord Jesus ascended to heaven he told his disciples to wait in Jerusalem for the coming of the Holy Spirit. Did the believers expect to be suddenly raptured at any moment or did they expect the Holy Spirit to come?
The answer is simple: they expected the Holy Spirit to come as promised by the Lord himself.

2. In Acts 23:11 the Lord appeared to Paul and told him he must go to Rome and witness. Now, did Paul expect to be raptured at any moment or did he expect to be witnessing in Rome in the days ahead?
He expected to be witnessing in Rome as his Messiah had told him. So was Paul a preacher of an any moment imminent rapture? Most certainly not.

3. In John 21:18 Jesus told Peter that he would live to be an old man. The scripture tells us in verse 19 Jesus said this signifying what manner of death Peter would suffer.

Do I really need to ask if Peter, throughout his life, was expecting the Lord to return and to rapture him at any moment?

Of course, he did not. His Messiah had told him to his face, he would grow old and die. How could anyone today preach and teach the lie that Peter believed and preached an any moment rapture? But sadly, many people do.

Logic tells us the church could not have been looking for an any moment, imminent rapture because Jesus Himself had predicted certain events would happen in the church.

The very fact that Jesus Himself predicted these events cancels any idea that the early church looked for an any moment imminent rapture.

They knew they had to see these events before Jesus returned for the church or Jesus would have been a false prophet.

Over we see the seven churches of Revelation. Most prophecy teachers tell us these also represent 7 ages through which the church will pass before the end. I have a question: If this is so, and it isn't accepted by everyone,... If the 7 churches of Revelation represent prophesies from the risen Lord Jesus for the 7 ages of church history.............

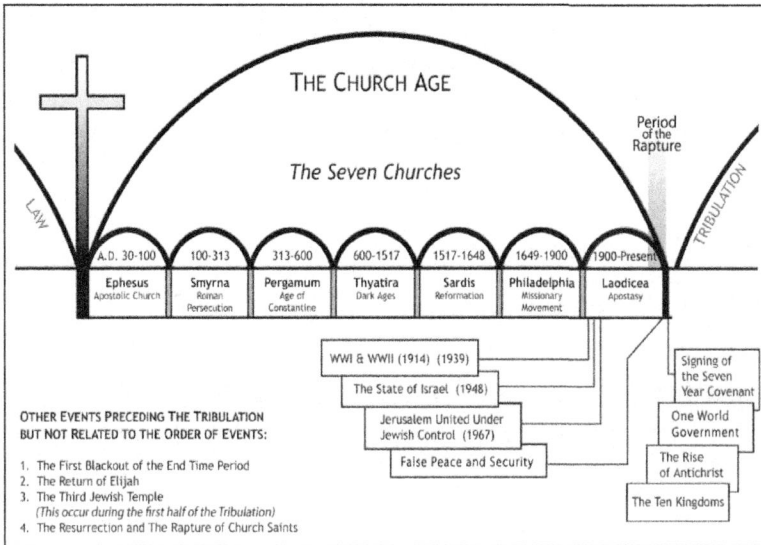

THE CHURCH AGE

The Seven Churches

LAW

Period of the Rapture

TRIBULATION

A.D. 30-100	100-313	313-600	600-1517	1517-1648	1649-1900	1900-Present
Ephesus Apostolic Church	Smyrna Roman Persecution	Pergamum Age of Constantine	Thyatira Dark Ages	Sardis Reformation	Philadelphia Missionary Movement	Laodicea Apostasy

WWI & WWII (1914) (1939)

The State of Israel (1948)

Jerusalem United Under Jewish Control (1967)

False Peace and Security

OTHER EVENTS PRECEDING THE TRIBULATION BUT NOT RELATED TO THE ORDER OF EVENTS:

1. The First Blackout of the End Time Period
2. The Return of Elijah
3. The Third Jewish Temple
   (This occur during the first half of the Tribulation)
4. The Resurrection and The Rapture of Church Saints

Signing of the Seven Year Covenant

One World Government

The Rise of Antichrist

The Ten Kingdoms

www.ltradio.org

How could He have returned <u>at any moment</u> for the last 2,000 years if all these predictions for the church age had to come to pass first?

Thus, the teaching that for the past 2,000 years the church expected an "any moment" secret rapture is simply not true.

It doesn't fit the facts of either church history or history revealed in scripture.

In his book "When the Trumpet Sounds"; Harvest House, p. 221, Gerald B. Stanton writes "Imminency inspires hope for the any-moment return of our Lord. Imminency is a concept that has been held by Christians throughout the church's history_and, yet, it has recently come under renewed attack by proponents of the pre-wrath rapture view. A denial of the

13

doctrine of imminency erodes biblical truth and undermines holy living in the anticipation of Christ's return."

Is this statement true? Has imminency been a belief held throughout the church's history?

Let's look at the early church Fathers. Did they expect to be rescued before the appearance of the Antichrist?

Justin Martyr, (100-165) Dialog with Trypho, CX "*[T]wo advents of Christ have been announced*: the one, in which He is set forth as suffering, inglorious, dishonored, and crucified; but the other, in which He shall come from heaven with glory, *when*
the man of apostasy, who speaks strange things against the Most High, shall venture to do unlawful deeds on the earth against us the Christians,..." (emphasis added)

Irenaeus (early 2nd Century To -202) Against Heresies Book V, XXVI ten kings, who have received no kingdom as yet, but shall receive power as if kings one hour with the beast. These have one mind, and give their strength and power to the beast. These shall make war with the Lamb, and the Lamb shall overcome them, because He is the Lord of lords and the King of kings." It is manifest, therefore, that of these [potentates], he who is to come shall slay three, and subject the remainder to his power, and that he shall be himself the eighth among them. And they shall lay Babylon waste, and burn her with fire, and shall give their kingdom to the beast, and put the Church to flight. After that, they shall be destroyed by the coming of our Lord". (Book 5, Chapter 26)
Tertullian (155-240) On the Resurrection of the Flesh

"In the Revelation of John, again, the order
of these times is spread out to view, which *'the souls of the
martyrs' are taught to wait for beneath the altar*, whilst they
earnestly pray to be avenged and judged: (taught, I say, to
wait), in order that the world may first drink to the dregs the
plagues that await it out of *the vials* of the angels, and that
the city of fornication may receive from the ten kings its
deserved doom, and *that the beast Antichrist with his false
prophet may wage war on the Church of God;,...*" (emphasis
added)

Hippolytus (170-235) Treatise on Christ and Antichrist, 61
"*That refers to the one thousand two hundred and threescore
days (the half of the week) during which the tyrant is to reign
and persecute the Church*, which flees from city to city, and
seeks concealment in the wilderness among the
mountains,...*" (emphasis added)

Victorinus (Died 303) Commentary on the Apocalypse,
"The little season signifies *three years and six months, in
which with all his power the devil will avenge himself under
Antichrist against the Church*." (emphasis added)

Reading the scriptures we have quoted above, and the
writings of the church Fathers, I am stunned that so many
fall for the tale told from many pulpits and prophecy
seminars today that the early church believed in an any
moment rapture.

Isn't it clear that they most definitely did not?

THE BLESSED HOPE

Tit 2:13 Looking for that blessed hope, and the glorious appearing of the great God and our Saviour Jesus Christ;

If the "Blessed Hope" is the secret pre-tribulation rapture of the church it is a hope that was unknown to the church for the first 1800 years until the teachings of John Nelson Darby come into prominence in the 1830's.

THE UNKNOWN DAY OR HOUR

Matthew 24:36 But of that day and hour knoweth no *man, no, not the angels of heaven, but my Father only.*

Which "day and hour" is the Lord Jesus speaking about?

Those who believe in a pre-tribulation rapture tell me "Jesus is speaking about the day of the pre-tribulation rapture. The timing of the pre-tribulation rapture is unpredictable" they say.

But if we read the text in context, it is clear Jesus is speaking about His post-tribulation coming, not a pre-tribulation Rapture.

He doesn't mention a pre-tribulation coming at all....

Mat 24:29-31 Immediately after the tribulation of those days shall the sun be darkened, and the moon shall not give her light, and the stars shall fall from heaven, and the powers of the heavens shall be shaken. And then shall appear the sign of the Son of man in heaven: and then shall all the tribes of the earth mourn, and they shall see the Son of man coming in the clouds of heaven with power and great glory. And he shall send his angels with a great sound of a trumpet, and they shall gather together his elect from the four winds, from one end of heaven to the other.

And just 5 verses later, Jesus says:

Mat 24:36 But of that day and hour knoweth no *man, no, not the angels of heaven, but my Father only.*

How can pre-tribulation rapture teachers have the effrontery to accuse cults such as the Jehovah's Witnesses of manipulating scriptures to suit their agenda and then take this verse where Jesus is speaking about his post-tribulation return and tell their congregations Jesus is alluding to a pre-tribulation secret rapture that he has not mentioned once and is found nowhere from Genesis to Revelation? The level of deception is nothing short of appalling. How people do not see through this manipulation of the word of God is almost beyond comprehension. With the technology we possess today and the number of bibles that are readily available online and in book form it is almost unforgivable that people should be so willing to blindly swallow this false teaching and scriptural juggling without so much as a pause in their thinking. This teaching in Matthew 24, Mark 13 and Luke 21 is what has become known as the Olivet Discourse when Jesus gave the clearest run down of future events leading to his return. But because he doesn't mention a pre-tribulation coming we are told he was not speaking to the church in this passage but to the Jews. My answer to that is another question: "Please can you tell me when wasn't he talking to the Jews?"

He was always talking to Jews. He lived in Israel where the Jewish people lived. He was a Jewish Rabbi. What is so special here that separates his sayings from the church to the Jewish people alone in this passage. The answer is there is nothing that would make anyone reading it conclude he was speaking to the Jewish people specifically. He was not speaking to a crowd. In fact, at this point, he was addressing his inner circle of friends.

Mark 13: 3 tells us he was privately speaking to Peter, James, John and Andrew. And all through his address, he continually says to them "when you see, when you see." As if he expected his followers to be around when the Antichrist appeared and at no time did he so much as hint they would be gone before this event. In fact, the Olivet Discourse reveals our Lord expected completely the opposite and his followers were to watch out for these things. Why then do we argue with the Messiah?

Another argument for a secret any moment rapture is given by quoting Luke 12:40: Be ye, therefore, ready also: for the Son of man cometh at an hour when ye think not.
This is not a clue to show us there will be a pre- tribulation rapture. The whole section this is found in must
be read in context. It is a command from the Lord to be ready

and prepared for his return and not to be lazy servants. It is very bad teaching to simply quote a verse without including the surrounding text.

THE DAY OF THE LORD

We are often taught the final 7 years are also known as the Day of the Lord as well as the tribulation. This is why many teach a pre-tribulation rapture: so we may avoid the Day of the Lord because we are not appointed to wrath.

I agree we are not appointed to his wrath. But let us search the scriptures to see if we can discover any clues regarding this terrible time of judgement and deliverance.

Isa 13:9-11 Behold, the Day of the Lord cometh, cruel both with wrath and fierce anger, to lay the land desolate: and he shall destroy the sinners thereof out of it. For the *stars of heaven and the constellations thereof shall not give their light: the sun shall be darkened in his going forth, and the moon shall not cause her light to shine.* And I will punish the world for their evil, and the wicked for their iniquity; and I will cause the arrogancy of the proud to cease, and will lay low the haughtiness of the terrible. (emphasis added)

Joel 2:10-11 The earth shall quake before them; the heavens shall tremble: *the sun and the moon shall be dark, and the stars shall withdraw their shining:* And the Lord shall utter his voice before his army: for his camp is very great: for he is strong that executeth his word: for the Day of the Lord is great and very terrible; and who can abide it? (emphasis added)

Joel 2:31

The _sun shall be turned into darkness, and the moon into_ _blood_, before the great and the terrible Day of the Lord come. (emphasis added)

Joel 3:14-15 Multitudes, multitudes in the valley of decision: for the Day of the Lord is near in the valley of decision. _The_ _sun and the moon shall be darkened, and the stars shall_ _withdraw their shining_ (emphasis added)

So from these scriptures, the prophets tell us the Day of the Lord will be heralded by certain cosmic signs. Jesus was the greatest of all the prophets, so where did Jesus place the signs preceding the Day of the Lord and the rapture? Let's listen to the master himself:

Mat 24:29-31 Immediately after the tribulation of those days shall the sun be darkened, and the moon shall not give her light, and the stars shall fall from heaven, and the powers of the heavens shall be shaken: And then shall appear the sign of the Son of man in heaven: and then shall all the tribes of the earth mourn, and they shall see the Son of man coming in the clouds of heaven with power and great glory. And he shall send his angels with a great sound of a trumpet, and they shall gather together his elect from the four winds,

from one end of heaven to the other. (emphasis added)

Jesus, the greatest prophet of them all, places the exact same heavenly signs preceding the Day of the Lord AFTER the tribulation and never before. So is the Day of the Lord the final 7 years? Not according to the Messiah himself. Who will you believe? Your favourite prophecy teachers or your Lord and Master?

What did Paul write regarding the rapture and the Day of the Lord?

1Th 4:16-18 For the Lord himself shall descend from heaven with a shout, with the voice of the archangel, and with the trump of God: and the dead in Christ shall rise first: Then we which are alive *and remain shall be caught up together with them in the clouds, to meet the Lord in the air: and so shall we ever be with the Lord.* Wherefore comfort one another with these words. (emphasis added)

These verses are known as one of the pillars of the pre-tribulation rapture. However, this is where most people stop reading. We must remember the letters of Paul never had verses. So we continue reading his letter

1 Thessalonians 5:1-4 But of the times and the seasons, brethren, ye have no need that I write unto you. For yourselves know perfectly that the <u>Day of the Lord</u> so cometh as a thief in the night. For when they shall say, Peace and safety; then sudden destruction cometh upon them, as travail upon a woman with child; and they shall not escape. But ye, brethren, are not in darkness, that that day should overtake you as a thief. (emphasis added)

This is very important because Paul is linking the Day of the Lord with the rapture and he is also telling the Thessalonians that the Day of the Lord will *not* take them by surprise. But Jesus placed the Day of the Lord AFTER the tribulation. It seems clear to me that there is no other route we can honestly take than to listen to Jesus and Paul and conclude the Day of the Lord takes place after the tribulation and that is where Jesus and Paul place the rapture.

Paul later states 2 events must take place before we are gathered to the Lord and the Day of Christ (Day of the Lord) begins.

2 Thess 2:1-3 Now we beseech you, brethren, by the coming of our Lord Jesus Christ, and by our gathering together unto him, that ye be not soon shaken in mind, or be troubled, neither by spirit, nor by word, nor by letter as from us, as that the Day of Christ is at hand. Let no man deceive you by any means: for that day shall not come, except there come a falling away first, and that man of sin be revealed, the son of perdition;

In more recent days some have attempted to say that the falling away mentioned here is, in fact, the pre-tribulation rapture. But the Greek word used here apostasia denotes a moving away from one set of beliefs to another and not a physical removal from one location to another i.e. heaven..

So Isaiah said: Isa 13:10 <u>For the stars of heaven and the constellations thereof shall not give their light: the sun shall be darkened in his going forth, and the moon shall not cause her light to shine</u>

Joel said: Joel 2:31 <u>The sun shall be turned into darkness, and the moon into blood,</u> before the great and the terrible Day of the LORD come.

Jesus said: Mat 24:29 Immediately after the tribulation of those days shall the <u>sun be darkened, and the moon shall not give her light, and the stars shall fall from heaven,</u>

Mat 24:31 And he shall send his angels with a great sound of a trumpet, and they shall gather together his elect from the four winds, from one end of heaven to the other. Paul agreed with Jesus: The rapture takes place at the same time as the Day of the Lord begins. 1Thess. 4/5, 2 Thess. 2: 1-3 What did John write in Revelation 6 / 7? Something very interesting.

As you see on the next page, the Olivet Discourse of Matthew 24 and the seals of Revelation 6 and 7 correspond exactly with each other. The seals in Revelation are not revealing to us simply the start of the tribulation, but they are if you will, chapter headings showing us events right up to the return of the Lord Jesus and our appearing in heaven after the tribulation.

THE OLIVET DISCOURSE MATTHEW 24	THE 6 SEALS REVELATION 6/7
1. FALSE MESSIAHS	1.WHITE HORSE: ANTICHRISTS
2. WARS	2.RED HORSE: WARS
3. FAMINES	3.BLACK HORSE: FAMINES
4. DEATH	4.PALE HORSE: DEATH
5.PERSECUTION	5.MARTYRS
6.COSMIC SIGNS PEOPLE MOURN;	6. COSMIC SIGNS: DAY OF HIS WRATH HAS COME
SOUND OF A TRUMPET; CHRIST GATHERS HIS ELECT	GREAT CROWD ARRIVES IN HEAVEN OUT OF THE GREAT TRIBULATION

NEITHER IN MATTHEW 24 OR REVELATION 6 / 7 DO WE FIND SO MUCH AS A HINT OF A PRE-TRIBULATION RAPTURE BUT SCRIPTURE REVEALS JUST THE OPPOSITE.
REVELATON 8 SHOWS US GOD'S JUDGEMENT &WRATH

DAY OF THE LORD RECAP:

So the prophets tell us there will be specific cosmic signs before the Day of the Lord, the day his wrath, is poured out on the earth.

Jesus, himself places the very same cosmic signs after the tribulation and at no time before. It is at that point, and that point only, he mentions gathering his elect.

The apostle Paul, in 1 Thessalonians 4 and 5 and 2 Thessalonians 2, links the rapture with the Day of the Lord and at no time earlier than this.

The seals in the book of Revelation correspond exactly with the signs given in Mathew 24 and Mark 13 thus revealing cosmic signs before God's wrath and before the great crowd arrives in heaven.

So it would seem from a simple reading of the word of God that the day of the Lord's wrath is preceded by cosmic signs; signs that are predicted by the prophets and the Messiah and the seals in the book of Revelation. The Messiah places these signs after the tribulation and Paul places the rapture of the church occurring at that same time while Revelation places the cosmic signs in the 6th seal and following this a great crowd arrives in heaven. To me it could not be clearer that the rapture takes place after the tribulation and before the wrath of God falls on the earth.

KEPT FROM THE HOUR

Rev 3:10 Because thou hast kept the word of my patience, I also will *keep thee from (Tereo ek)* the hour of temptation, which shall come upon all the world, to try them that dwell upon the earth. (emphasis added)

Pre-tribulation rapture teachers tell us this verse is a promise to believers of a physical removal from the planet to heaven before the appearance of the Antichrist and the onset of the tribulation.

But is it? The key phrase is "keep thee from" or Tereo ek in Greek. Does this mean a physical removal or does it mean something else? In John 17 we have the record of Jesus' prayer for his disciples. He prays to his Father: John 17:15 I pray *not that thou shouldest take them out of the world,* but that thou shouldest *keep them from (Tereo ek)* the evil. (emphasis added).

In this prayer, Jesus uses the same terms translated later into Greek "tereo ek". It is abundantly clear he is not asking the Father to remove his disciples from the planet. In fact, he prays for them not to be removed from the earth. Rather, he asks that they be kept "from the evil." In other words, it is a prayer for protection. Like a boxer in a fight, Jesus is asking that they do not "throw in the towel" and give up.

We must also remember to whom this letter was first written: to the Philadelphian church in Asia Minor in the first century.

Were they raptured out of the way of danger? Of course not, so why take a letter to a church of the 1st century, a letter that gave a promise of perseverance in a coming time of trouble and transfer it 20 centuries forward to the last days church and change its promise of perseverance into a promise of physical removal from the planet?

The church in Philadelphia did suffer persecution under the Roman emperor Trajan in 98 AD. This persecution of Christians lasted for over a century. But at the end of the persecution the church was still standing strong.

I decided to check how Greek language experts translated this verse. One again, it was a real eye-opener for me:

Goodspeed translates 3:10- "Because you have kept in mind the message of what I endured. I will also keep you safe in the time of testing that is going to come upon the whole world, to test the inhabitants of the earth."

Moffatt- "Because you have kept the word of my patient endurance, I will keep you safe through the hour of trial which is coming upon the whole world to test the dwellers on earth."

Fausett- "so as to deliver thee out of, not to exempt from temptation."

Swete- "to the Philadelphia Church the promise was an assurance of safe keeping in any trial that might supervene."

Zahn- "Jesus will requite him for this when He preserves him at the time of the great temptation that is to come and test the inhabitants of the earth,.."

Robert Gundry- "to keep or protect in a sphere of danger, and that because ek means emergence out from within, the combination of the two Greek words (TEREO EK) means to protect believers in a sphere of danger (the tribulation period), with a final emergence out from within this sphere."

"A final emergence out from within this sphere" takes us back to Revelation 7:9 After this I beheld, and, lo, a great

The multitude, which no man could number, of all nations, and kindreds, and people, and tongues stood before the throne, and before the Lamb, clothed with white robes, and palms in their hands.

Do you see, friends? The pre-tribulation rapture theory is just that: a theory and nothing more because it has not one verse in the entire bible to support it.

THE TWO WITNESSES

Many believe the two witnesses who appear in the final 7 years will be possibly Moses and Elijah due to the miracles God performed through them. Moses turned the waters to blood and Elijah calling down fire from heaven.

Many others believe the witnesses may be Enoch and Elijah because the bible states all men are appointed to die once and neither Enoch or Elijah died but were taken to heaven without seeing death.

The Jewish people also believe Elijah must come before the Messiah appears. What has the appearance of Elijah (the two witnesses) to do with the Day of the Lord? The answer is a problem for those who believe the final 7 years are the day of the Lord's wrath because God tells us in Mal 4:5-6

Behold, I will send you Elijah the prophet before the coming of the great and dreadful Day of the Lord: And he shall turn the heart of the fathers to the children, and the heart of the children to their fathers, lest I come and smite the earth with a curse.

Pre-tribulation teaches there are no signs indicating the rapture is near. Yet we are told we leave before the Day of the Lord which pre-tribulation says runs through the entire final 7 years.

If the final 7 years are, in fact, the Day of the Lord, then we should expect Elijah to appear before that awesome day. Wouldn't that be a sign the rapture is near? Anyone spotted Elijah yet?

CHURCH ABSENT FROM MOST OF REVELATION

Because the word "church" or "churches" is absent from 18 of Revelation's 22 chapters it is believed the church must be in heaven during these 18 chapters.

This is an argument from silence.

It is very dangerous to create a doctrine from silence. But, actually, the word "church" isn't mentioned as being in heaven either.....so where is she?

When the text mentions "saints" we are told this refers to "tribulation saints", those people who are converted after the rapture but are NOT part of the church! But, of course, as with most pre-tribulation teaching, there is no scripture at all that says this.

We are told the bulk of Revelation concerns events that take place *after* the church is raptured and the world enters the final 7 years before Christ's visible return.

We are also told by many teachers that the church is not mentioned in Revelation until chapter 19. But this is not true. The "bride" is mentioned, but not the word "church." However, if we allow that this is the church we still have a problem.

Here's why. If the church is in Heaven during the majority of the book of Revelation and the saints mentioned as being on earth are tribulation saints converted after the removal of the church to heaven, but who are not part of the church, can someone explain to me the event following the Millennial reign of Christ?

Rev 20:7 And when the thousand years are expired, Satan shall be loosed out of his prison, And shall go out to deceive the nations which are in the four quarters of the earth, Gog and Magog, to gather them together to battle: the number of whom *is as the sand of the sea.* And they went up on the breadth of the earth, and compassed the camp of the saints about, and the beloved city: and fire came down from God out of heaven and devoured them.

Did you notice the church is still not mentioned so where is the church?? In revelation 20, after the 1,000-year reign of Christ on earth, the word "church" is still absent from the text. We are told the saints are on earth with Christ but still there is no mention of the church! And according to pre-tribulation teaching the "saints" are those converted after the church has been raptured.

So after 1,000 years where is the church?

Unless the "saints" mentioned throughout Revelation are the church. Not raptured until after the tribulation just as Jesus promised in Matthew 24:31, Mark 13 etc.

Incredibly, if we adhere to the pre-tribulation view of the saints throughout Revelation, we discover in chapter 20, not the church on earth reigning with Christ at the end of the 1,000 years but so-called "tribulation saints."

According to the pre-tribulation rapture theory because the word "church" is not mentioned in the text she is absent from the earth and in heaven. So following the pre-tribulation argument, and being consistent, when reading Revelation 20, we are forced to say the church is, presumably, still in heaven and has been separated from Christ, who has been reigning on earth for 1,000 years.....with the tribulation saints and NOT the church!!! Simply because "church" is still not in the text.

We know the church will rule with Christ.

But how do we account for the word "church" being absent from the text through the tribulation and the Millennium of Revelation 20?

Unless ....

The saints seen throughout Revelation are, in fact, what they have been all through the New Testament..... The church, finally suffering through the tribulation, raptured after the tribulation and eventually ruling and reigning with Christ from Jerusalem where they are attacked by the world at the end of the 1,000-year reign.

Either the saints in Revelation are people converted after the rapture and they will rule with Christ on earth while the church remains absent from the text because she is in heaven or these saints are the church suffering through the tribulation, raptured after the tribulation as the Day of the Lord begins. Then returning with Christ and ruling with Him on earth for 1,000 years.

We cannot interpret "saints" as "tribulation saints" for several chapters and then suddenly turn them into "church saints" in chapter 20 in order to squeeze the text into our theology and have the church ruling with Christ.

Our theology has to fit the text.

Not the other way around.

Dan 7:18 But the saints of the most High shall take the kingdom, and possess the kingdom for ever, even for ever and ever. (Isn't this the church?)

Dan 7:19 Then I would know the truth of the fourth beast, which was diverse from all the others, exceeding dreadful, whose teeth *were of iron, and his nails of brass; which devoured, brake in pieces, and stamped the residue with his feet;* Dan 7:20 And of the ten horns that *were in his head, and of the other which came up, and before whom three fell; even of that horn that had eyes, and a mouth that spake very great things, whose look was more stout than his fellows.*

Dan 7:22 Until the Ancient of days came, and judgment was given to the saints of the most High; and the time came that the saints possessed the kingdom. (Isn't this the church also?)

If the saints who possess the kingdom in verse 18 are the Church and the saints to whom judgement and the kingdom are given in verse 22 are the Church, also, then can someone tell me who the saints are right in the middle of this chapter in Dan 7:21 I beheld, and the same horn made war with the saints, and prevailed against them; (Who then are these saints?)

In 14 of the 27 books of the New Testament, we read the word "Saints" and it always refers to the church.

Until we come to the 27th book.

The book of Revelation.

Then the "saints" miraculously become tribulation saints who are converted after the rapture but are not part of the church.

Please note the following verses:

Rev 14:12 -13 Here is the patience of the saints: here *are they that keep the commandments of God, and the faith of Jesus. And I heard a voice from heaven saying unto me, Write, Blessed are the dead which die in the Lord from henceforth: Yea, saith the Spirit, that they may rest from their labours; and their works do follow them.*

This is during the tribulation.

Let's use some simple logic:

If I "keep the commandments of God" and "keep the faith of Jesus" and "die in the Lord" doesn't that make me a Christian? Of course, it does.

And if people in the tribulation "keep the commandments of God", "keep the faith of Jesus" and "die in the Lord" surely they must, by definition, be Christians?

And if that is so, doesn't that mean they are part of the church?

Then doesn't simple logic show clearly the church is on earth in the tribulation?

And if that is so why are we continually taught the church has to be raptured *before* the tribulation?

What does Paul say about the dead in Christ? When are they raised?

1Th 4:14-17 For if we believe that Jesus died and rose again, even so them also that are fallen asleep in Jesus will God bring with him. 1Th 4:15 For this we say unto you by the word of the Lord, that we that are alive, that are left unto the coming of the Lord, shall in no wise precede them that are fallen asleep. For the Lord himself shall descend from heaven, with a shout, with the voice of the archangel, and with the trump of God: and the <u>dead in Christ shall rise</u>

first; then we that are alive, that are left, shall together with them be caught up in the clouds, to meet the Lord in the air: and so shall we ever be with the Lord.

There is no time given. However, there is one Greek word used here that could help us.

PERELEIPO

This word occurs only twice in the entire New Testament ....and only in 1 Thessalonians 4.

It can also mean Survived

Another translation would read:

"We which are alive and have survived shall not prevent those who are asleep in Jesus. Then, we which are alive and have survived shall be caught up together with Him in the clouds.

Survived what? I have no proof but could it possibly be the tribulation and persecution?

RAPTURE / HARPAZO

Harpazo" - "To be caught away, seize, pulled up, taken by force, snatched away" (Vine's)

Latin "rapare" from which we get the word "rape."

When such an event takes place it is usually with noise as when the crowd wanted to make Jesus their king and would have taken him by force. John 6:15

Or when the crowd threatened to take Paul by force Acts 23:10 and the Romans had to take action and rescued him from the mob by lifting him up above the crowd.

It is violent; it is often noisy.

KLEPTO / STOLEN SECRETLY

The Greek word Klepto (Strong's Number 2813) means to steal secretly. It is where we get our word "kleptomaniac."

Saint Paul COULD have used this word in Thessalonians to indicate a SECRET RAPTURE. However, he didn't. He used Harpazo, not Klepto.

Instead, the Holy Spirit decided to use a word that denotes violence, force and noise.

Does Harpazo sound like a secret rapture before the tribulation? Or does it sound like a violent rescue of the surviving saints after the tribulation as Christ returns in power and visible glory to pour out his wrath upon unrepentant mankind? Something akin to the following verses:

Mat 24:27-31 For as the lightning cometh out of the east, and shineth even unto the west; so shall also the coming of the Son of man be. And he shall send his angels with a great sound of a trumpet, and they shall gather together his elect from the four winds, from one end of heaven to the other.

1Th 4:16-17 For the Lord himself shall descend from heaven,

with a shout, with the voice of the archangel, and with the trump of God: and the dead in Christ shall rise first; then we that are alive, that are left, shall, together with them be caught up in the clouds, to meet the Lord in the air:

Aither or Aer?

Two miles is just over 3,218.7 meters   or 10,560 feet .

Mount Olympus is   2,919 meters high or 9,577 feet.

An ancient Greek standing on the summit of Mount Olympus would look up into the sky and the thinner atmosphere and say "aither." Pointing down toward the earth he would say "aer" meaning the lower denser atmosphere.

Paul knew this very well and of course so did the Holy Spirit who inspired him to write his epistles.

So which word did Paul use in the following verse: 1Th 4:17 then we that are alive, that are left, shall, together with them be caught up in the clouds, to meet the Lord in the air:

He, under the inspiration of the Holy Spirit, wrote "aer"!

So, according to Saint Paul and the Holy Spirit, the Lord Jesus will descend with hordes of angels, a loud shout of command and a blast of a trumpet. Millions of dead and living believers will rise to meet the Lord in the air. And it takes place less than 2 miles above the earth! Pre-tribulation teachers tell us this will be "secret." No one will hear or see this apart from believers.

ARE YOU KIDDING ME??

Where does the bible say this will be unseen, and silent? Nowhere!

Now do you see why Paul wrote: "Harpazo" (violent, noisy) and not "Klepto" (silent, stolen secretly)? There is no room for a pre-tribulation secret rapture in these verses.

THE LAST TRUMPET

THE LAST TRUMPET

PRE-TRIB
LAST TRUMP

POST- TRIB
LAST TRUMP

7 YEARS

ANTICHRIST

1 Corinthians 15:51-52
Last Trumpet

Revelation 11:15-19
1 Corinthians 15:51-52
Last Trumpet

Strongs 2078 "final, uttermost."
How many "Trumpets "
can there be after the "Last Trumpet"?

Pre-tribulation teachers place the last trumpet of 1 Corinthians at the rapture of the church when all dead and living believers are caught up together to be with Christ as he returns secretly to take them to heaven.

They readily agree there is another trumpet at the end of the tribulation when the dead are again raised and Christ returns visibly this time. According to Strongs 2078 translation of the word "Last", it means "final, the uttermost."

How can there be a "Last trumpet" before the tribulation at the pre-tribulation rapture and another "Last trumpet" blown at the end of the tribulation?

Well-known teachers of the pre-tribulation rapture get around this by saying the "Last Trumpet" of 1 Corinthians 15 is for believers.

The "Last Trumpet" of Revelation 11 at the end of the tribulation (and in Matthew 24:31) is for the unsaved. But this is injected into the text.

There is not the slightest suggestion these two trumpets are not one and the same, sounded at the rapture after the tribulation.

When does the 7th angel of Revelation sound the trumpet? Read on...

Mat 24:31 And he shall send his angels with a <u>great sound of a trumpet</u>, and they shall gather together his elect from the four winds, from one end of heaven to the other.

1Co 15:52 In a moment, in the twinkling of an eye, at the last trump: <u>for the trumpet shall sound</u>, and the dead shall be raised incorruptible, and we shall be changed.

1Th 4:16 For the Lord himself shall descend from heaven, with a shout, with the voice of the archangel, and with the trump of God and the dead in Christ will rise…

Rev. 11:15-18 And the <u>seventh angel sounded;</u> and there were great voices in heaven, saying, The kingdoms of this world are become the kingdoms of our Lord, and of His Christ; and He shall reign for ever and ever. And the four and twenty elders, which sat before God on their seats, fell upon their faces, and worshipped God, Saying, We give thee thanks, O Lord God Almighty, which art, and wast, and art to come; because thou hast taken to thee thy great power, and hast reigned. And the nations were angry, and thy wrath is come, and the time of the dead, that they should be judged, and that thou <u>shouldest give reward unto thy servants the prophets, and to the saints, and them that fear thy name, small and great;</u> and shouldest destroy them which destroy the earth. (emphasis added)

Do you see it is at this time when the trumpet sounds the dead are raised in 1 Corinthians 15 and 1 Thessalonians 4 and the time comes for them to be rewarded in Revelation 11? This is taking place at the same time at the end of the tribulation just before the wrath of the Lord falls on the earth.

THE MARRIAGE OF THE LAMB: WHEN DOES IT TAKE PLACE?

According to the secret rapture pre-tribulationists the Marriage of the lamb, when Christ welcomes his bride the church into heaven, takes place before the final 7 years begin and lasts right up until the Second Coming at the end of the 7years. But what does the bible say?

The bible is a Middle Eastern apocalyptic book and as such it tends to jump forward and back throughout the narrative. One chapter may show the reader a scene in heaven and then move on. A later chapter returns to the earlier event and reveals more detail not shown previously.

So as we read Revelation we discover this tendency to hop back and forth. See the events depicted below:

THE MARRIAGE OF THE LAMB WHEN DOES IT TAKE PLACE?

- Rev 14:8 Angel declares Babylon is fallen ⟷ Rev. 19:2 The Harlot (Babylon) is fallen

- Rev. 14:14-16 Christ gathers His elect ⟷ Rev. 7:9; 19:2-9 Great crowd appears in Heaven

- You fill in the dots......
- Rev. 19:7-9 The Marriage has come

- Rev. 14:17-20 Angels gather the wicked to Armageddon ⟷ Rev. 19:18-21 Christ defeats Antichrist at Armageddon

Does anyone see the Rapture or the Marriage of the Lamb at the start of the tribulation or at the end in this text?

It should be clear that the arrival of the great crowd in heaven does not happen until the end of the tribulation as shown earlier in the explanation of the seals in Revelation 6 / 7 and Matthew 24. Then the Marriage of the of the lamb takes place and rewards are given and at no time earlier. We do not read about any of these events happening until after the tribulation.

One argument against a post-tribulation rapture is the notion that once the Antichrist is made known half way through the 7 years all one has to do is count the days until the end of the final three and a half years and you will know when Christ is returning.

This reveals a lack of understanding Jesus' words in the Olivet Discourse when he stated concerning the tribulation: Matthew 24:22 And except those days should be shortened, there should no flesh be saved: but for the elect's sake those days shall be shortened.

In other words, this may mean the tribulation will not run the full length of three and a half years, but will be cut short for some reason.

Cut short by how much we do not know. And it is, for this reason, we will not be able to count the days off to the return of the Lord. But we do know he has not left us completely in the dark. He said after the tribulation when we see the cosmic signs heralding the Day of the Lord we are to look up because he is on his way, praise his wonderful name.

So let us review this short explanation of the post-tribulation rapture of the church.

- Pre-trib says the church has always believed in imminence.
- Post-trib, history and logic show the church never believed in the imminent return of Christ.

- Pre-trib says Jesus gathers the believers before the tribulation.

- Jesus, the prophets, the Apostles and the early church all state he comes after the tribulation.

- There is not one mention by any of them of a rapture before the tribulation.

- Pre-trib says the final 7 years are the "Day of the Lord's Wrath"

- Jesus, the Prophets, Paul and John in Revelation, all place the cosmic events preceding the Day of the Lord AFTER the tribulation and at no time before.

- Pre-trib states there are two "Last Trumpets" One at the pre-trib rapture and one at the Second coming after the tribulation.

  The Greek Scriptures show clearly there can only be one "Last Trumpet" and it is sounded after the tribulation

- The scriptures show clearly Elijah the prophet will appear before the "Day of the Lord"

- Pre-trib seems to ignore this scripture because if the final 7 years are the "Day of the Lord" Elijah must appear before the 7 years even begin. This would also be a sign of the coming rapture and pre-trib states there are no signs warning of the rapture.

- Pre-trib believes The "Marriage Supper of the Lamb" takes place during the whole 7 years following the pre-trib rapture.

- Scriptures, as well as Revelation 19, places the "Marriage Supper of the Lamb" immediately around the time of the battle of Armageddon after the tribulation.

- Post-trib believes the rapture takes place after the tribulation just as Jesus, the Apostles and the early church stated.

- The Day of the Lord occurs after the tribulation, after the rapture as the Prophets, Jesus and the Apostles and Early church stated.

- Post-trib believes There is only one last trumpet, blown at the rapture, after the tribulation as Jesus and the Apostles stated.

- Post-trib believes Elijah the prophet will possibly come as one of the two witnesses, before the Day of the Lord, sometime during the final 7 years, as scripture clearly shows the Day of the Lord begins AFTER the tribulation.

- Post-trib believes the saints of revelation are in fact the church. There is absolutely no scriptural reason to believe they are anything other than born-again believers in the Lord Jesus and, therefore, members of the church.

- Post-trib believes:

- The Marriage Supper of the Lamb takes place at the end of the tribulation around the time of the battle of Armageddon as scripture says in Revelation 19.

- It is mentioned at no time before.

THIS LOOKS LIKE A POST-TRIBULATION RAPTURE TO ME.

I realise this may raise more questions than answers and I have no intention of upsetting or angering my fellow Christians. Please e-mail me if you have a question. I may not be able to answer you but may be able to put you in touch with someone else who can.

May the Lord Bless you as we await his return.

Contact Bob Mitchell: bobmitchell777@yahoo.com

Printed in Great Britain
by Amazon